s should be addressed to:

cational Series, Inc.
ys Park Drive
ew York 11797

andard Book
7-8
ess Catalog Card

ess Cataloging
ta

I. Title. II. Series.
1.5'3 83-22458

G
6 5 4 3 2 1

Credits

Photography
Color photographs: Matthew Klein
Food stylist: Andrea Swenson
Stylist: Linda Cheverton

Author Janeen Sarlin teaches cooking classes in New York City and owns the cooking school Cooking with Class, Inc.

Cover and book design Milton Glaser, Inc.

Series editor Carole Berglie

Lunches to Go

by Janeen Sarlin

BARRON'S
Woodbury, New York · London · Toronto · Sy

Se

All
No
in any
xerog
incorp
system,
written

All inquirie
Barron's Ed
113 Crossw
Woodbury,
International S
No. 0-8120-555
Library of Congr
No. 83-22458

Library of Cong
in Publication Da
Sarlin, Janeen.
Brown bag lunches
(Easy cooking)
Includes index.
1. Lunchbox cookery.
TX735.S26 1984 6
ISBN 0-8120-5557-8
PRINTED IN HONG KON
4 5 6   490   9 8 7

INTRODUCTION

Before the advent of plastic wrap, sandwich baggies, plastic containers, and lightweight insulated tote bags, the thought of a "take-it-with-you-lunch" was a poorly wrapped, squashed sandwich in a brown paper bag with a hole in it.

Today, the lunchbox or brown bag goes to grade school, college, the factory, office, beach, and library. And it comes in all shapes and sizes. Some use a brown paper bag, a "proper" picnic basket with all the trimmings, a black metal box with thermos on top, a pretty insulated bag, a large plastic food storage bag, a briefcase, or even a pocket. But wherever you eat your lunch or however you "tote" it with you, you'll find this book will give you easy ways to perk up your favorite foods and suit your personal style.

Last night's dinners create great lunchtime ideas: Russian Roast Beef; Steak Tex-Mex style; New England Autumn Special; Mediterranean Pocket. Some are transformed and others purposely left over. The Scandinavian Glazed Ham Loaf is perfect for dinner with the reserved stuffing from the California Potato Crisps. You'll probably find that more lunch ideas are just as good for dinner!

When marketing for the week's lunchboxes, buy the best of the season's fruit and vegetables. If the recipe calls for a fresh peach and the month is March, substitute a banana or whatever fruit is available. Green beans taste terrific during summer months; broccoli and cauliflower are great in the fall; both can be interchanged to take advantage of the season. Crisp romaine leaves make an excellent substitute for bread. The summertime offers a bountiful selection; however, your winter lunch bag can include a tangerine, dried fruits, or a grapefruit as well as the standard apple.

Food is only part of lunch. Take a walk to the park, find a lovely tree to sit under, and have your lunch there. Or go to your friends' office for lunch and then take a brisk walk around the block. If it's raining, visit a museum or library and have lunch when you return. Another good idea is to do isometrics in the hallway.

Presentation is an important part of the lunchbox that most people neglect. Colorful napkins help to brighten any lunch. Buy a few large, bright, easy-care cloth napkins on sale. Tuck one under your chin to catch a crumb from falling on your new shirt or tie. Place another napkin under your lunch as a placemat. Add sparkle to your brown bag with multicolored paper napkin. Line a cakebox with a yellow paper dinner napkin and tuck a blue one in for fingers. If a fork and knife are needed, take good ones along. The bottom drawer of your desk is the perfect place for a pretty wine glass for your iced tea.

Interesting and pretty portable lunch foods needn't be expensive. For example, peeled broccoli stems cut with an oriental slant are a crunchy variation from carrot and celery sticks. A melon half with zig-zag cuts creates a useful yet pretty "basket" for fruit and yogurt. The empty plastic yogurt cups are perfect for a sticky sweet pickle garnish or a bit of tangy mustard sauce for dipping.

Dare to be adventuresome and your ordinary lunchbox will become extraordinary!

UNDERSTANDING THE RECIPE ANALYSES

For each recipe in this book, you'll note that we have provided data on the quantities of protein, fat, sodium, carbohydrates, and potassium, as well as the number of calories (kcal) per serving. If you are on a low-calorie diet or are watching your intake of sodium, for example, these figures should help you gauge your eating habits and help you balance your meals. Bear in mind, however, that the calculations are fundamentally estimates and are to be followed only in a very general way. The actual quantity of fat, for example, that may be contained in a given portion will vary with the quality of meat you buy or with how much care you take in skimming off cooking fat. If you are on a rigid diet, consult your physician. The analyses are based on the number of portions given as the yield for the recipe, but if the yield reads, "4 to 6 servings," we indicate which number of servings (4, for example) was used to determine the final amounts.

SPECIAL BREAD RECIPES
The following bread recipes will deliciously complement the lunch makings in this book. Make them in the evening or on a weekend to have the breads ready for slicing during the week.

RYE BREAD

YIELD
2 round loaves

Per slice
calories 95, protein 3 g, fat 1 g, sodium 212 mg, carbohydrates 18 g, potassium 54 mg

TIME
45 minutes preparation
2 hours, 40 minutes rising
45 minutes baking
1 hour cooling

INGREDIENTS
2 packages (1/4 ounce each) active dry yeast
3 tablespoons sugar
2 tablespoons caraway seeds
1/4 teaspoon baking soda
1 tablespoon salt
2 cups beer
2 tablespoons butter

1 cup whole-wheat flour
2 cups rye flour
3 cups white flour

Mix yeast, sugar, caraway seeds, baking soda, and salt together in large mixing bowl. In saucepan, warm beer and butter until butter is melted, but not boiling. Pour beer mixture into yeast mixture and mix thoroughly. Add whole-wheat flour using a mixing-kneading motion or the dough hook on an electric mixer.

Mix in rye flour and finally white flour, mixing well after each addition. Turn onto floured surface. Cover and let rest for 10 minutes. Knead 10 to 15 minutes or until smooth and elastic. Place in greased bowl. Cover and let rise in a warm place until doubled in bulk (approximately 1 1/2 to 2 hours). Punch dough down, shape into round loaves, and place on a greased cookie sheet and let rise until doubled in size (approximately 35 to 40 minutes).

Heat oven to 375 degrees, and bake for 35 to 45 minutes or until loaf sounds hollow when tapped on the bottom. Cool on rack. Slice for almost any sandwich; this bread also tastes good toasted and with butter for breakfast!

OVERNIGHT ROLLS

YIELD

24 rolls or 2 loaves

Per roll

calories 150, protein, 5 g,
fat 2 g, sodium 285 mg,
carbohydrates 28 g,
potassium 48 mg

TIME

35 minutes preparation
Overnight rising
25 minutes baking
15 minutes cooling

INGREDIENTS

2 packages (¼ ounce each) active dry
   yeast
1 teaspoon sugar for proofing
2¼ cups lukewarm water
½ cup sugar
8 cups sifted flour
1 tablespoon salt

2 tablespoons lard or butter, melted
   and cooled
2 eggs, beaten

Place the yeast, sugar, and ¼ cup warm water in small bowl to proof for 15 to 20 minutes. In a large mixing bowl, combine remaining water, sugar, and 4 cups flour. Beat well. Stir in yeast mixture; add salt, lard, eggs, and rest of flour, mixing until smooth. Do not add more flour. Place dough in a greased mixing bowl, cover with a large inverted plastic bag, and place in the refrigerator overnight.

The next morning, shape dough into rolls, or divide in half and place in 2 greased 9 by 3 by 2-inch bread pans or onto 2 baking sheets. Cover with plastic wrap and let rise 45 minutes for loaves, 30 minutes for rolls.

Heat oven to 400 degrees. Bake loaves or rolls for 10 minutes, reduce heat to 350 degrees, and bake until evenly browned and bread sounds hollow when tapped on bottom (rolls take total of 20 to 25 minutes; 30 to 40 minutes longer for loaves). Cool bread on racks. Fantastic as sandwich roll.

HERBED BISCUITS

YIELD

12 biscuits

Per biscuit

calories 177, protein 2 g,
fat 10 g, sodium 347 mg,
carbohydrates 17 g,
potassium 52 mg

TIME

15 to 20 minutes
   preparation
12 minutes baking

INGREDIENTS

2 cups sifted flour
3 teaspoons baking powder
1 teaspoon salt
½ teaspoon sugar
¼ cup minced fresh chives
¼ cup minced fresh parsley
6 tablespoons butter, cut into slices
⅔–¾ cup heavy cream

Sift flour, baking powder, salt, and sugar together in the bowl of a food processor. Add the herbs and process 2 to 3 pulses. Place butter in bowl and process until dough resembles coarse meal. Stir in cream with a fork. Place dough on a floured board and knead 2 to 3 times, then roll out with a rolling pin to a ½-inch thickness. Cut circles with a 3-inch cookie or biscuit cutter. Place circles on an ungreased cookie sheet. Heat oven to 450 degrees and bake biscuits for 10 to 12 minutes or until golden brown.

YIELD

2 servings

Per serving
calories 527, protein 39 g,
fat 27 g, sodium 397 mg,
carbohydrates 30 g,
potassium 301 mg

TIME

15 minutes preparation

INGREDIENTS

2 sesame pita breads, split
2 tablespoons mayonnaise
I whole chicken breast, cooked and
    boned
2 green bell pepper rings
2 red bell pepper rings
2 ounces provolone cheese
I teaspoon olive oil

Cut pita breads in half ① and lightly toast each pocket.

Spread mayonnaise on inside of each pocket.

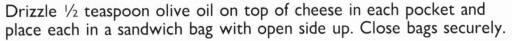

Cut chicken breasts in half, then slice into thin slices ② and place I half in each pocket.

Place I green pepper ring and I red pepper ring on top of chicken.

Shred provolone cheese ③ and tuck in pockets.

Drizzle ½ teaspoon olive oil on top of cheese in each pocket and place each in a sandwich bag with open side up. Close bags securely.

Pack along black olives and a fresh peach for dessert.

YIELD

2 servings

Per serving
calories 313, protein 17 g,
fat 11 g, sodium 803 mg,
carbohydrates 36 g,
potassium 649 mg

TIME

5 minutes preparation

INGREDIENTS

1 tablespoon butter
4 slices pumpernickel bread
1 can (2 ounces) boneless and skinless
   sardines
2 teaspoons lemon juice
½ teaspoon freshly ground black
   pepper
2 slices red onion
4 slices ripe tomato

Lightly butter pumpernickel bread.

Drain off oil from sardines ①, open each lengthwise ②, and place on plate.

Drizzle lemon juice over sardines and season with freshly ground black pepper.

On each of 2 slices of bread place 1 red onion slice, pushed out into rings ③.

Place 2 slices each of tomato on top of the onion slices and season with pepper to taste.

Place sardines on remaining slices of bread. Join with other slices to make a sandwich and cut into triangle halves. Wrap individually to carry to school or work.

YIELD

2 servings

Per serving
calories 674, protein 28 g,
fat 23 g, sodium 517 mg,
carbohydrates 89 g,
potassium 476 mg

TIME

8 minutes preparation
2 hours marinating

INGREDIENTS

¹/₃ pound fresh bay scallops
3 tablespoons lime juice
¹/₈ teaspoon white pepper
1 scallion, minced
1 small tomato, chopped
2 black olives, sliced
¹/₂ hot pepper, minced (optional)
2 tablespoons olive oil
Pinch of cumin
2 hero rolls
2 lettuce leaves

Wash and drain scallops ①. Toss in shallow glass bowl with lime juice and pepper. Cover and marinate 2 hours or overnight in refrigerator.

Drain scallops, reserving juice, and toss with scallion, tomato, black olives, and red pepper.

Mix olive oil with 1 tablespoon of reserved juice. Add cumin and toss with the scallop mixture ②. Taste and correct seasonings. (This can be done ahead of time and refrigerated covered.)

Split each hero roll and pull out some of insides ③.

Place a lettuce leaf on each roll. Top with scallops. Replace top of hero. Wrap each in plastic wrap and take along an orange for dessert.

CARIBBEAN FRUIT BASKET

YIELD

2 servings

Per serving
calories 227, protein 8 g,
fat 2 g, sodium 105 mg,
carbohydrates 47 g,
potassium 1160 mg

TIME

20 to 25 minutes
preparation

INGREDIENTS

1 medium cantaloupe
⅓ cup blueberries
⅓ cup green seedless grapes
1 cup vanilla yogurt

Cut melon in half with a big zig-zag pattern ①; scoop out seeds ②. Cut fruit away from rind ③, leaving each melon half as a basket.

Cube melon pulp, and place in bowl. Mix in blueberries and grapes.

Dress fruit with yogurt, then place fruit in melon baskets. Cover tightly with plastic wrap.

Serve with plantation chips. Garnish with fresh mint leaves.

NOTE *Any fresh fruit in season can be substituted.*

YIELD

2 servings

Per serving
calories 632, protein 23 g,
fat 28 g, sodium 1830 mg,
carbohydrates 68 g,
potassium 364 mg

TIME

15 minutes preparation

INGREDIENTS

16 fresh thin asparagus spears
16 thin slices baked ham
½ cup Dijon-style mustard
2 tablespoons mayonnaise
1 loaf French bread

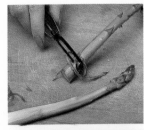

Peel asparagus spears from tip down ① and snap off tough ends ②. Wash and drain dry.

Wrap a slice of ham around each spear ③, leaving the tips exposed. Place 8 each in 2 food storage bags.

Mix mustard and mayonnaise together. Divide into 2 small plastic containers with lids.

At lunch, dip the wrapped asparagus spears into the sauce and eat with crusty French bread. Pack a container of fresh strawberries for dessert.

NOTE You may substitute thicker asparagus spears, but gently parboil for 4 minutes before wrapping with ham.

YIELD

2 servings

Per serving

calories 222, protein 22 g,
fat 13 g, sodium 609 mg,
carbohydrates 3 g,
potassium 383 mg

TIME

10 minutes preparation

INGREDIENTS

1 can (7 ounces) solid white tuna in
   water, drained
2 scallions, sliced
1 tablespoon mayonnaise
1 tablespoon olive oil
1 tablespoon lemon juice
1/8 teaspoon freshly ground black
   pepper
2 tablespoons drained capers
6 large romaine leaves, washed and
   drained

Flake tuna with a fork into a small mixing bowl ①. Add the scallions, mayonnaise, olive oil, lemon juice, and pepper ② and mix well. Stir in capers ③. Place in a plastic container.

Take romaine leaves along and use them as "boats" for open-face sandwiches. Serve with fresh cherry tomatoes and a nectarine.

YIELD

2 servings

Per serving (1 of each)
calories 300, protein 7 g,
fat 13 g, sodium 882 mg,
carbohydrates 40 g,
potassium 401 mg

TIME

5 minutes preparation

CUCUMBER SANDWICHES

2 teaspoons butter, softened
¼ teaspoon chopped fresh dill
2 slices white bread, crusts removed
1 kirby cucumber, peeled and thinly sliced

RADISH SANDWICHES

2 teaspoons butter, softened
2 slices pumpernickel bread
4 radishes, thinly sliced
Approximately ¼ teaspoon coarse salt

WATERCRESS SANDWICHES

2 teaspoons butter, softened
⅛ teaspoon celery salt
2 slices whole-wheat bread, crusts removed
4 to 5 sprigs fresh watercress, stems removed

For cucumber sandwiches, mix butter and dill together ①. Spread on bread and top with sliced cucumbers. Cut into small squares. Wrap securely.

For radish sandwiches, spread butter on bread ②. Top with sliced radishes, season with coarse salt, and cut into small squares. Wrap securely.

For watercress sandwiches, mix butter and celery salt together. Spread on bread, top with watercress leaves, and cut into small squares ③. Wrap securely.

Pack a variety of little sandwiches for each person. Include a fresh peach for dessert.

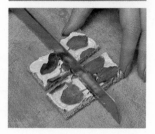

YIELD

2 servings

Per serving
calories 816, protein 12 g,
fat 51 g, sodium 817 mg,
carbohydrates 82 g,
potassium 560 mg

TIME

25 minutes preparation
1½ hours baking
1 hour cooling

INGREDIENTS

3 ounces cream cheese
¼ cup chopped walnuts
5 to 6 stuffed olives, sliced

FRUIT-NUT LOAF

2 cups finely chopped assorted dried
    fruit (raisins, apricots, prunes, etc.)
1½ cups all-purpose flour
3 teaspoons baking powder
½ teaspoon salt
¾ cup sugar

¾ cup sweet butter, cold
2 eggs
1 tablespoon milk
1½ teaspoons almond extract

Prepare the fruit-nut loaf first. Preheat the oven to 350 degrees. Place fruit in a bowl. Pour enough boiling water over fruit to cover and soak 10 utes. Drain off water, shake off excess moisture, and allow fruit to drain in a colander set over a plate while you prepare the batter.

Place flour, baking powder, salt, and sugar in a bowl of a food processor and mix for 1 or 2 pulses.

Cut butter into tablespoon-size pieces. Place in bowl and process 7 or 8 pulses or until mixture is consistency of bread crumbs.

Remove mixture to a mixing bowl and stir in drained fruits.

In small bowl, beat eggs with fork. Add milk and almond extract. Stir liquid into flour and fruit mixture ① and beat thoroughly. The batter will be stiff.

Spread batter into 1 greased 12¾ × 3¾-inch long loaf pan ② or 2 smaller 8¼ × 4¼-inch pans. Bake for 1½ hours or until a toothpick inserted in center comes out clean ③. Cool in pan 10 to 15 minutes, then remove to cool on a rack. Wrap loaf in foil and freeze or refrigerate. Loaf makes enough for 6 to 8 regular sandwiches or 16 to 18 tea or cocktail sandwiches.

To make sandwich, cut 4 slices from loaf. Mix cream cheese with walnuts and olives.

Spread a slice of fruit-nut loaf with the cream cheese mixture. Place another slice on top. Cut into desired shapes and wrap. Take along celery and carrot sticks.

PARISIAN POULET

YIELD

2 servings

Per serving
calories 644, protein 51 g,
fat 25 g, sodium 976 mg,
carbohydrates 49 g,
potassium 428 mg

TIME

15 minutes preparation

INGREDIENTS

2 shallots
1 loaf French bread
8 leaves bibb lettuce
1 large whole chicken breast, cooked
   and sliced
1 tablespoon Dijon-style mustard
4 ounces gruyère cheese, shredded

Chop the shallots ①. Split bread in half lengthwise. Pull out some of centers ②.

Place lettuce on 1 half; top with sliced chicken. Spread mustard over other half ③. Sprinkle with chopped shallots and top with shredded gruyère cheese.

Replace top of loaf and divide in half. Wrap and serve with chilled white wine and red seedless grapes.

SCANDINAVIAN GLAZED HAM LOAF

YIELD

8 servings

Per serving (loaf only)
calories 357, protein 18 g,
fat 17 g, sodium 392 mg,
carbohydrates 32 g,
potassium 351 mg

TIME

30 minutes preparation
35 minutes cooking
1 hour cooling

INGREDIENTS

3/4 pound veal, pork, and beef, ground
    together
3/4 pound boiled ham, coarsely ground
1 egg
3/4 cup milk
1 cup soft bread crumbs
1/4 cup grated onion
1/4 cup chopped fresh parsley
1/2 teaspoon pepper
1 cup brown sugar
1 1/4 teaspoons dry mustard
1/4 cup cider vinegar

FOR 2 SANDWICHES

1 teaspoon mustard mixed with 1
    teaspoon of glaze
4 slices rye bread
2 slices ham loaf

Preheat oven to 375 degrees. Turn ground meat into large bowl. Add ground ham and, with hands or wooden spoon, mix in egg, milk, bread crumbs, onion, parsley, and pepper ①. Form into loaf and place in oiled 8¼ × 4¼-inch loaf pan ②.

Mix sugar, mustard, and vinegar in small saucepan. Bring to boil and boil 5 minutes. Pour hot glaze over ham loaf ③ and bake 30 to 35 minutes or until loaf is glazed and brown and juices run clear. Cool in pan, then refrigerate covered. This loaf can be frozen, also. It is great to serve for dinner (serves 4), then can be used the next day to make sandwiches.

To make sandwiches, spread mustard-glaze mixture on bread. Top with ham loaf slices. Wrap sandwiches and take along sweet pickles and fresh plums.

YIELD

2 servings

Per serving
calories 474, protein 34 g,
fat 25 g, sodium 1168 mg,
carbohydrates 30 g,
potassium 565 mg

TIME

15 minutes preparation
2 minutes cooling

INGREDIENTS

1 can (7 ounces) solid white tuna in
  water
1 small onion, chopped
1 stalk celery, chopped
2 to 3 tablespoons mayonnaise
¼ cup tiny canned peas
4 slices whole-wheat bread
2 slices American cheese

Flake tuna with a fork into a small bowl ①.

Add onion, celery, and mayonnaise and mix well.

Stir in peas. Spread tuna salad on 2 slices of bread ② and place a slice of cheese on top of each ③. Run under broiler for 2 minutes or microwave for 30 seconds or until cheese is melted. Top with remaining slices of bread and serve hot with crispy delicious apple or wrap and take along to enjoy cold.

BRITISH BEEF ROLL

YIELD

2 servings

Per serving
calories 301, protein 22 g,
fat 8 g, sodium 397 mg,
carbohydrates 30 g,
potassium 283 mg

TIME

8 minutes preparation

INGREDIENTS

2 teaspoons butter
½ teaspoon prepared horseradish
2 onion rolls, split
4 slices roast beef
2 radishes, sliced
2 slices raw onion

Mix butter and horseradish together ①. Split onion rolls ②, and spread with horseradish mixture. Top each sandwich with roast beef, radishes and onion slice ③. Pack for later, with celery sticks and golden delicious apples.

YIELD

2 servings

Per serving
calories 694, protein 41 g,
fat 41 g, sodium 345 mg,
carbohydrates 40 g,
potassium 471 mg

TIME

10 minutes preparation

INGREDIENTS

1½ cups diced cooked chicken
¼ cup salted peanuts
3 scallions, sliced
¼ cup mayonnaise, approximately
¼ teaspoon curry powder
1 tablespoon chutney
2 large pita breads

Mix chicken pieces, peanuts, and scallions with mayonnaise, curry powder, and chutney ①. Blend well. Taste and correct seasoning. Split pita breads ② and stuff with chicken salad ③. Wrap securely and pack along with a banana or green seedless grapes.

YIELD

2 servings

Per serving
calories 370, protein 23 g,
fat 8 g, sodium 448 mg,
carbohydrates 53 g,
potassium 563 mg

TIME

8 to 10 minutes
preparation

INGREDIENTS

1 red delicious apple
Lemon juice
1 tablespoon mayonnaise
4 slices homemade bread (pumpkin,
   if you have it)
4 slices turkey breast or leftover dark
   meat
2 tablespoons cranberry relish

Slice apple ① and dip in lemon juice ② to keep from darkening.

Spread mayonnaise on bread. Top with turkey ③, apple slices, and relish. Wrap well and take along a thermos of chilled apple cider.

JAPANESE SHRIMP AND SLAW

YIELD

2 to 3 servings

Per serving
calories 451, protein 24 g,
fat 31 g, sodium 482 mg,
carbohydrates 21 g,
potassium 833 mg

TIME

15 minutes preparation
2 minutes cooking
30 minutes chilling

INGREDIENTS

$^1/_2$ pound shrimp in the shell, cleaned
2 cups water
1 tablespoon rice wine vinegar
2 to 3 cloves
2 small onions, 1 sliced and 1 minced
$^1/_2$ small head cabbage
2 tablespoons chopped fresh parsley
$^1/_3$ cup mayonnaise (approximately)
Pinch of salt
$^1/_2$ teaspoon black pepper
1 green pepper, slivered

Clean shrimp ①. Bring water, vinegar, cloves, and sliced onion to a boil in saucepan. Boil 2 minutes, then add shrimp and cook 1 to 2 minutes or until shrimp just turn pink. Drain and rinse with cold water. Remove shells. Refrigerate until ready to use.

Shred cabbage in food processor ②. Mix in minced onion and parsley. Add enough mayonnaise to bind ③ and season with salt and pepper.

Toss shrimp with slaw and place in plastic containers. Top with green pepper slivers and cover securely.

Pack with crackers or cookies.

YIELD

2 servings

Per serving
calories 423, protein 34 g,
fat 17 g, sodium 454 mg,
carbohydrates 31 g,
potassium 350 mg

TIME

15 minutes preparation

INGREDIENTS

¼ head iceberg lettuce
2 ounces monterey jack cheese
2 hard rolls
6 slices steak or London broil
2 teaspoons taco sauce

Shred lettuce ① and cheese ②. Set aside for assembly.

Split rolls ③. Place 3 slices each of steak on each bottom half, and top with lettuce and cheese. Season with taco sauce, and place tops of rolls on each sandwich. Wrap individually and serve with corn chips.

YIELD

5 servings

Per serving (pinwheel roll only)
calories 552, protein 42 g, fat 34 g, sodium 791 mg, carbohydrates 18 g, potassium 630 mg

TIME

25 minutes preparation
1½ hours cooking

INGREDIENTS

2 pounds ground beef
2 eggs
1 cup chopped onions
¼ cup chopped fresh parsley
4 slices rye bread with caraway seeds, soaked in ½ cup milk, then squeezed dry
2 teaspoons black pepper
1½ cups canned sauerkraut, rinsed, drained, and squeezed dry
¾ cup shredded swiss cheese
Mustard

Preheat oven to 350 degrees. Lightly oil a baking sheet.

Mix meat, eggs, onions, parsley, bread, and pepper. Place meat mixture on a sheet of plastic wrap and flatten evenly with a wet spatula to a rectangle about 10 by 15 inches ①.

Place drained sauerkraut evenly over the meat.

Top sauerkraut with cheese ② and roll up, jellyroll style, using plastic wrap to guide you ③. Roll onto 15 × 11 × 1½-inch baking pan and bake uncovered in oven for 1½ hours. Cool to room temperature and/or refrigerate until ready to cut. This loaf can also be frozen.

To make sandwiches, spread mustard on slices of rye bread, top with pinwheel slices, and cover with another bread slice. Wrap and serve with cherry tomatoes and a juicy apple. (Great for a picnic too.)

RUSSIAN FRUIT 'N CHEESE

YIELD

2 servings

Per serving
calories 639, protein 38 g,
fat 23 g, sodium 1258 mg,
carbohydrates 75 g,
potassium 983 mg

TIME

15 minutes preparation

INGREDIENTS

1 teaspoon candied citron
2 to 3 red plums
1 pound cottage cheese
2 tablespoons sour cream
¼ cup golden raisins
¼ cup slivered almonds
¼ pound fresh sweet cherries
   (approximately)
2 pumpernickel rolls

Dice the citron ①. Quarter the plums ②.

Combine cottage cheese with sour cream ③. Add raisins, almonds, and citron and mix well.

Place cheese mixture in 2½-pound plastic containers with lids. Arrange plums around edges and place cherries on top. Cover container and serve with pumpernickel rolls.

YIELD

2 servings

Per serving
calories 364, protein 7 g,
fat 26 g, sodium 199 mg,
carbohydrates 31 g,
potassium 440 mg

TIME

10 minutes preparation

INGREDIENTS

2 large ripe pears
1 ounce blue cheese, softened
1 ounce sweet butter, softened
1/4 cup chopped pistachio nuts

Cut pears in half lengthwise, leaving stem and skin on ①. Remove core ② without detaching stem ③. Scoop out a bit more fruit.

Mix cheese and butter together until smooth. Place half the mixture in the center of each pear half and "glue" the halves together.

Roll the edges in chopped pistachios. Place in refrigerator 20 to 30 minutes to firm up or place in portable cooler to keep cold until you are ready to eat. Serve with prosciutto-wrapped Italian breadsticks.

YIELD

2 servings

Per serving
calories 325, protein 9 g,
fat 18 g, sodium 197 mg,
carbohydrates 37 g,
potassium 471 mg

TIME

10 minutes preparation

INGREDIENTS

2 large eating apples, such as red
  delicious
4 tablespoons peanut butter
2 tablespoons grated coconut
2 tablespoons golden raisins

Halve apples lengthwise ①. Remove cores and a bit of the apple pulp inside ②.

Mix peanut butter, coconut, and raisins, then fill core of apples ③ and place halves back together. Wrap securely. Serve with candied pineapple slices and Hawaiian punch.

ITALIAN DRUMSTICKS

YIELD

2 servings

Per serving
calories 479, protein 48 g,
fat 21 g, sodium 440 mg,
carbohydrates 20 g,
potassium 447 mg

TIME

10 minutes preparation
45 minutes cooking

INGREDIENTS

6 chicken drumsticks
Approximately 1 cup dry bread
   crumbs
1/4 cup grated parmesan cheese
Pinch of black pepper
Pinch of paprika
1 teaspoon Italian herbs
1/4 cup milk

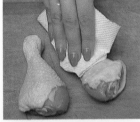

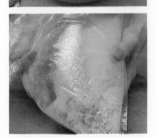

Preheat oven to 350 degrees. Line a baking sheet with aluminum foil.

Wash and pat chicken dry ①.

Mix bread crumbs, cheese, pepper, paprika, and Italian herbs in a double plastic bag.

Dip chicken in milk ②, then place in bag with crumbs and shake ③. Place chicken on baking sheet and bake in oven for approximately 45 minutes, or until browned and juices run clear when stuck with a fork.

Wrap 3 drumsticks for each person. Serve with a buttered Italian roll and a red pepper cut into quarters.

MIDWESTERN DEVILED EGGS

YIELD

6 servings

Per serving
calories 309, protein 12 g,
fat 28 g, sodium 632 mg,
carbohydrates 3 g,
potassium 165 mg

TIME

45 minutes preparation
25 minutes cooking

INGREDIENTS

1 dozen small or medium eggs
6 tablespoons unsalted butter,
  softened
2 tablespoons mayonnaise
1 tablespoon Dijon-style mustard
1 teaspoon salt
1 teaspoon pepper

GARNISHES

1/4 cup chopped fresh parsley
1/4 cup chopped scallions, both green
  and white parts
1/4 cup crumbled bacon bits

Place eggs in a saucepan with enough water to cover by 1 inch. Cover and bring to a boil. Remove from heat and let stand 20 minutes. Cool eggs in cold water, then tap the shells against side of pan to crack. Peel eggs, and cut in half. Remove yolks to a sieve placed over a mixer bowl.

Set whites aside. Push yolks through sieve ① and, with beaters, beat in softened butter, mayonnaise, mustard, salt, and pepper ②. Taste and correct seasoning according to your palate.

Place eggs back together with some of stuffing along edges ③. Roll 4 eggs in chopped parsley, 4 eggs in chopped scallion, and 4 eggs in crumbled bacon. Wrap 2 eggs of each type for each person and serve with rolls, a slice of cold luncheon meat, and carrot sticks.

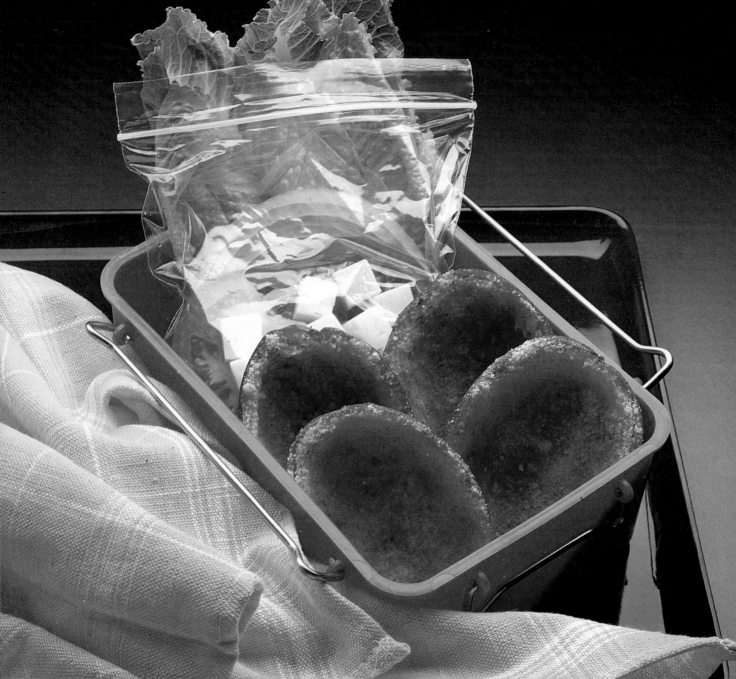

CALIFORNIA POTATO CRISPS

YIELD

2 servings

Per serving
calories 487, protein 26 g,
fat 29 g, sodium 727 mg,
carbohydrates 31 g,
potassium 883 mg

TIME

10 minutes preparation
5 to 10 minutes baking

INGREDIENTS

8 large baking potatoes
½ cup freshly grated parmesan
   cheese
Dash of paprika
4 lettuce leaves
1 ripe tomato, sliced
½ large sweet onion, sliced
1 tablespoon mayonnaise
¼ pound monterey jack cheese, cubed

Preheat the oven to 375 degrees.

Scrub potatoes and prick skin with fork. Bake for 1 hour or until done. Remove from oven; cut potatoes in half lengthwise (use pot holder for hands) ①. While still hot, remove inside of potato ② and reserve for dinner or another use. Place skins back on baking sheet and sprinkle with cheese and paprika ③. Return to oven for 5 to 10 minutes or until skins are crispy and cheese is melted.

Place lettuce leaves in separate plastic container or a double strength food storage bag. Top with tomato slices, onion slices, and a dollup of mayonnaise. Sprinkle cubed cheese on top and close the bag. Carry potato crisps in separate bag. (These are great for snacks, too.)

GERMAN LIVERWURST LOAF

YIELD

2 servings

Per serving
calories 1241, protein 51 g,
fat 78 g, sodium 3098 mg,
carbohydrates 81 g,
potassium 737 mg

TIME

30 minutes preparation
4 hours chilling

INGREDIENTS

1 pound German-style liverwurst,
  removed from casing
4 scallions, both green and white
  parts minced
2 sweet gerkins, minced
2 tablespoons minced fresh parsley
2 hard-cooked eggs, chopped
1 teaspoon mayonnaise
½ teaspoon ground coriander
1 tablespoon prepared mustard
2 hero loaves

Break up liverwurst with fork in a bowl. Add scallions, gerkins, parsley, eggs, mayonnaise, coriander, and mustard and mix well. Taste and correct seasoning.

Remove one end of the hero roll. Pull out center of bread ① and reserve for bread crumbs.

"Stuff" the liverwurst pâté into the bread, using a rubber scraper or knife ②. Replace the end and wrap in plastic wrap ③. Refrigerate to firm up.

Before wrapping for lunch, cut slices with a sharp knife and place in original shape. Wrap in aluminum foil or plastic wrap. Serve with cold beer.

YIELD

2 servings

Per serving
calories 632, protein 49 g,
fat 34 g, sodium 574 mg,
carbohydrates 30 g,
potassium 600 mg

TIME

25 minutes preparation

INGREDIENTS

2 cups diced cooked chicken
1 cup cooked broccoli flowerets
2 scallions, both green and white
   parts sliced
Pinch of sugar
Dash of soy sauce
1/4 teaspoon chopped fresh gingerroot
1 tablespoon rice wine vinegar
2 tablespoons vegetable oil
Pinch of black pepper
1 1/2 cups cooked Chinese noodles,
   cooled and drained

Mix chicken, broccoli, and scallions in a bowl ①.

In small jar with lid, place sugar, soy sauce, ginger, vinegar, oil, and pepper. Cover and shake well. Pour over chicken ② and mix well.

Distribute Chinese noodles in the bottom of 2 plastic containers ③. Put chicken and broccoli mixture on top and close lids.

Serve with drained mandarin oranges or fresh pineapple spears and a rice cake.

YIELD

1 serving each

Per serving (1 of each)
calories 407, protein 30 g,
fat 17 g, sodium 565 mg,
carbohydrates 37 g,
potassium 1438 mg

TIME

10 to 12 minutes
preparation

CUCUMBER CROCODILE

1 long cucumber

BUMPS ON A LOG

2 stalks celery, washed and trimmed
3 tablespoons crunchy peanut butter
¼ cup raisins

CARROT CIGARS

4 slices salami
2 slices turkey
2 slices roast beef
2 carrots, peeled and washed
Mustard

For the Cucumber Crocodile, wash cucumber and trim one end to form a nose ①.

Make slices down rest of body ②, but cut only ⅞'s of way through. Form mouth by cutting out triangle ③. Cut slant slice to form tail.

For the Bumps on a Log, fill centers of the celery stalks with peanut butter. Sprinkle raisins on top.

For the Carrot Cigars, wrap salami, then turkey and lastly roast beef around carrots very tightly. Serve with a roll.

Three ideas for a kid's lunch, these pleasers are sure to be a hit. Wrap whichever you choose to make and slip it into a school lunchbox.

27

YIELD

2 servings

Per serving
calories 364, protein 33 g,
fat 8 g, sodium 554 mg,
carbohydrates 39 g,
potassium 705 mg

TIME

10 minutes preparation

INGREDIENTS

6 slices roast beef
4 slices pumpernickel bread
1 tablespoon prepared horseradish
10 slices red beets, drained
2 tablespoons sour cream

Place roast beef on 2 slices of bread. Sprinkle with a bit of horse-radish ①. Top with sliced beets ② and dress with a dollup of sour cream ③. Top with remaining slices and serve with borsch or fresh orange juice.

YIELD

2 servings

Per serving
calories 481, protein 7 g,
fat 40 g, sodium 167 mg,
carbohydrates 28 g,
potassium 411 mg

TIME

10 minutes preparation

INGREDIENTS

2 large tart apples, such as granny
   smith
4 ounces boursin or herbed cheese,
   softened
2 ounces shelled pecans, chopped

Cut apples into eighths ① and core them, leaving bottom skin to hold apple together ②.

Mix cheese with pecans, then fill apple center and between the petals with cheese mixture ③. Close slightly and wrap in plastic wrap. Serve with croissant or brioche and glass of wine.

LAPLAND BARS

YIELD

16 bars

Per serving
calories 144, protein 3 g,
fat 7 g, sodium 56 mg,
carbohydrates 19 g,
potassium 92 mg

TIME

15 minutes preparation

INGREDIENTS

1/2 cup sugar
1/2 cup light corn syrup
1/2 cup crunchy peanut butter
1/2 teaspoon vanilla extract
3 cups popped popcorn
1 cup natural grated coconut
1/2 cup shelled peanuts (unsalted)

Lightly butter an 8-inch square cake pan.

Combine sugar and light corn syrup in a saucepan. Bring to boil and boil for 2 1/2 minutes.

Stir in peanut butter and vanilla, and mix until smooth.

Place popcorn, coconut, and peanuts in a large bowl. Then pour peanut butter mixture over nuts and corn. Stir with wooden spoon to coat all the popcorn.

Press mixture firmly into buttered cake pan. Cool and cut into 2-inch squares while still warm. Delicious for all seasons and ages.

OLD ENGLISH LEMON POUND CAKE

YIELD

8 to 10 servings

Per serving (8)
calories 715, protein 10 g,
fat 39 g, sodium 169 mg,
carbohydrates 81 g,
potassium 119 mg

TIME

15 minutes preparation
1 hour 15 minutes baking

INGREDIENTS

3/4 pound sweet butter
2 cups sugar
7 eggs
2 1/2 cups all-purpose flour
2 teaspoons baking powder
Grated rind of 1 lemon
Juice of 1 large lemon

Preheat oven to 375 degrees. Lightly grease and flour 2 8 1/4 × 4 1/4-inch loaf pans.

Cream butter and sugar until light and fluffy.

Add eggs, one by one, beating well after each addition.

Sift flour and baking powder together and mix into batter.

Stir in rind and lemon juice.

Turn batter into loaf pan. Tap bottom to settle into pan and bake for 1 hour to 1 hour 15 minutes, or until cake tester comes out clean. A crack is characteristic.

Cool cake in pan for 10 to 15 minutes, then remove and cool on rack. Store in the refrigerator. This cake freezes very well. It can be dessert for *any* lunchbox just as is or frosted with simple butter cream frosting.

HAWAIIAN ORANGE COOKIES

YIELD

60 cookies

Per cookie
calories 41, fat 2 g,
sodium 28 mg,
carbohydrates 5 g,
potassium 10 mg

TIME

25 minutes preparation
10 minutes baking
Overnight chilling

INGREDIENTS

¼ cup butter
¼ cup solid vegetable shortening
½ cup white sugar
2 tablespoons brown sugar
½ teaspoon lemon extract
1 tablespoon grated orange rind
1 egg
1½ cups all-purpose flour
¼ teaspoon salt

1½ teaspoons baking powder
1 cup flaked coconut

Cream butter, shortening, and sugars together until fluffy. Add extract, orange rind, and egg. Add flour, salt, baking powder, and cocunut. Mix well. Shape dough into 2 rolls approximately 1½ × 7 inches on waxed paper. Wrap tightly in plastic wrap and chill in refrigerator overnight or freeze.

Next day, or when you want fresh cookies, preheat oven to 400 degrees and cut ¼-inch slices and bake until edges are brown (10 minutes). Store in airtight container. These cookies are a favorite for lunchbox as well as tea time treats.

ALL-AMERICAN CHOCOLATE CHIP CHEWS

YIELD

12 large squares

Per square
calories 333, protein 2 g,
fat 19 g, sodium 160 mg,
carbohydrates 39 g,
potassium 125 mg

TIME

5 minutes preparation
25 minutes baking

INGREDIENTS

1 cup butter, softened
1 cup brown sugar
2 cups all-purpose flour
1 teaspoon almond extract
¾ cup chocolate chips
¼ cup flaked coconut

Preheat oven to 325 degrees. Grease a 9-inch square cake pan.

Cream butter and sugar together until light and fluffy. Mix in flour and extract. Stir in chips and coconut. Pat into baking pan and bake approximately 35 minutes or until center is firm and before cookies are browned.

Cut into squares while hot. All ages love these bars.

INDEX